BOOK ANALYSIS

Written by Lina Duarte Tovar
Translated by Rebecca Neal

Portnoy's Complaint

BY PHILIP ROTH

PHILIP ROTH

- **Born in Newark (New Jersey) in 1933.**
- **Literary awards:**
  - Three-time winner of the PEN/Faulkner Award for Fiction, 1994, 2001 and 2007 (for *Operation Shylock*, *The Human Stain* and *Everyman*)
  - Pulitzer Prize in Fiction, 1998 (for *American Pastoral*)
  - Gold Medal in Fiction from the American Academy of Arts and Letters, 2001
  - Prince of Asturias Award for Literature, 2012
- **Notable honours:**
  - National Medal of Arts, 1998
  - Honorary Doctor of Letters degree from Harvard University, 2003
- **Notable works:**
  - *Letting Go* (1962), novel
  - *The Breast* (1972), novella
  - *Operation Shylock* (1993), novel

- *American Trilogy* (comprising *American Pastoral*, 1997; *I Married a Communist*, 1998; and *The Human Stain*, 2000), novels

The American writer Philip Roth is the second son of an American Jewish family that originated from the Ukrainian-Polish region of Galicia. He grew up in the mainly Jewish neighbourhood of Weequahic in Newark, New Jersey, and this had a major influence on much of his work. He studied English at Bucknell University in Lewisburg, Pennsylvania, before earning an M.A. in English Literature from the University of Chicago and teaching English there. He then taught creative writing at the University of Iowa and Princeton University, and comparative literature at the University of Pennsylvania. He retired from teaching in the early 1990s.

At the University of Chicago, Roth met two other influential writers, namely Saul Bellow, who shared his Jewish origins, and Margaret Martinson, who went on to become his first wife. His dysfunctional relationship with Martinson and subsequent divorce had a major impact on his writing, and she provided the inspiration for a number of his female characters, including Mary Jane Reed in *Portnoy's Complaint* (1969). This was Roth's most successful novel to date: although he had first found fame with the short story collection *Goodbye Columbus* (1959), which won the 1960 US National Book Award for Fiction, he had failed to repeat this success with his subsequent works, namely *Letting Go* (1962) and *When She Was Good* (1967).

The 1970s was a decade of major creative experimentation for Roth, as he dabbled in a range of genres, including political satire with *Our Gang* (1971) and Kafkaesque absurdism with *The Breast* (1972), and introduced one of the recurring characters in his works, namely Nathan Zuckerman, the protagonist of books including *The Ghost Writer* (1979), *Zuckerman Unbound* (1981), *The Anatomy Lesson* (1983), *The Counterlife* (1986) and *Exit Ghost* (2007). Roth's most successful decade was arguably the 1990s, when he wrote *Operation Shylock* (1993), *Sabbath's Theater* (1995) and his so-called *American Trilogy*, comprising the Pulitzer Prize-winning *American Pastoral* (1997), *I Married a Communist* (1998) and *The Human Stain* (2000).

Although he has never won the Nobel Prize in Literature, arguably the most prestigious award for a living writer, he is probably the most decorated American writer of his generation – no small feat, considering that his contemporaries include such illustrious figures as Thomas Pynchon, Don DeLillo and Cormac McCarthy. In his extensive body of work, a clear progression is visible from his earliest novels and short stories, which tend to focus on the conflict between traditional Jewish morality and young American Jews' search for an identity of their own, and his later books, which often reflect on his role as a writer and a son, and on the relationships between art and life and illness and death. Roth received the Prince of Asturias Award for Literature in 2012, and shortly before the ceremony (which he could not attend because of a back operation), he told the French magazine *Les Inrockuptibles* that he had retired from writing and that *Nemesis* (2010) would be his last book.

ROTH'S AUTOBIOGRAPHICAL WRITING

Roth has written two volumes of memoirs, namely *The Facts: A Novelist's Autobiography* (1988) and *Patrimony: A True Story* (1991). *The Facts* recounts his life from his childhood to his rise to become a renowned but controversial writer, while *Patrimony* focuses on his father's death from a brain tumour and received the 1991 National Book Critics Circle Award.

PORTNOY'S COMPLAINT

A HEADY MIXTURE OF RAGE AND LUST

- **Genre:** novel
- **Reference edition:** Roth, P. (1994) *Portnoy's Complaint*. New York: Vintage.
- **1ˢᵗ edition:** 1969
- **Themes:** the tension between the Jewish and non-Jewish worlds, sexuality, shame, the role of women

Portnoy's Complaint is Philip Roth's fourth book, and was the novel that catapulted him to fame and made him one of the most controversial writers of the second half of the 20th century. This reputation stretched beyond his native America to countries as far afield as Australia, where the novel was initially banned due to its sexually explicit content.

The novel takes the form of a monologue delivered by Alexander Portnoy during his psychoanalysis sessions with Doctor Spielvogel.

Portnoy is a Jewish lawyer who works as the Assistant Commissioner for the City of New York Commission on Human Opportunity, and tells Spielvogel (and, by extension, the reader), about the different stages of his life so far and the influence his Jewish upbringing has had on him.

FROM PAGE TO SCREEN

Portnoy's Complaint was adapted into a film directed by Ernest Lehman and starring Richard Benjamin and Karen Black in 1972.

SUMMARY

The novel is structured around Portnoy's sessions with his psychoanalyst, which means that the narrative does not progress in chronological order, but jumps between the past (Portnoy's childhood) and the present (his adulthood). He is trying to explore his actions and feelings in order to cure his malaise, which his psychiatrist dubs "Portnoy's Complaint", meaning "[a] disorder in which strongly-felt ethical and altruistic impulses are perpetually warring with extreme sexual longings, often of a perverse nature" (Front Matter). In this section, we have arranged the key events in the protagonist's life in chronological order for the sake of clarity.

EARLY YEARS

From the novel's first pages, we are aware of the "ubiquity" (pp. 4 and 5) of Alex's mother Sophie. At the age of five, Alex thinks that all his female teachers are his mother in disguise, checking that he is behaving himself and spying on the way he acts when she is not around. Alex does not grow out of this paranoia, which follows him into adulthood. His earliest memories reveal a world that is shaped by love, but also by fear and overprotectiveness.

Alex is the youngest son of a Jewish couple, Alex and Sophie, who see him as a kind of rough diamond who can be polished into a great man, not only in professional terms but also in his personal life. His father works hard during the week to provide for his family, which means that Sophie spends more time with the children, cooks for them and makes sure that they are clean so that they will not pick up germs and fall ill. However, in spite of her good intentions, her treatment of her children can be brutal: if Alex's behaviour is not completely impeccable at all times, she kicks him out of the house and threatens not to let him back in. When he does not want to eat, she sits next to him with a large bread knife and tells him that children who do not eat do not grow, and asks him whether he wants to be a successful man or an abject failure when he grows up. He feels threatened by the knife and decides to eat, knowing that he will have to be strong if he wants to survive.

ADOLESCENCE

Alex's teenage years are hard for him. Like many 14-year-old boys, his life revolves around masturbating and rebelling against authority. However, somewhat unusually, the most exciting part of masturbation for him is the fear that his parents or someone else will catch him doing it. He frequently masturbates in the urinals at school, uses objects such as fruit, meat, bottles and items of his sister's clothing, masturbates to a strict schedule, and gets a particular thrill from doing it in the bathroom during family meals. One of his most memorable episodes is when his mother knocks insistently on the door to ask if he has diarrhoea from eating a forbidden food and demands to inspect the contents of the toilet; meanwhile, he is frantically masturbating on the other side of the door. In another sign of his burgeoning exhibitionism, he masturbates next to a sleeping woman on a bus from New York to Newark, in the knowledge that she could wake up at any moment. He wonders whether his compulsive need to masturbate is normal and whether other teenagers feel the same way.

Alex frequently clashes with his father, the main authority figure in his life and the person who is responsible for passing down the Jewish tradition. In particular, Alex is very vocal about his atheism, belief in science and left-wing political leanings. Moreover, at an important Jewish celebration he reduces his father to tears when he lambasts him for being ignorant and says that his ancestors' journey to the United States means nothing to him.

Alex becomes even more determined to defy his parents after they force his cousin Heshie to break up with his girlfriend, who is a *shikse* (a term for a non-Jewish woman), in order to maintain the family's honour. The fact that Heshie meekly follows their orders serves to intensify Alex's resentment towards his family and moves him to lead a double life: he is both a star student who throws occasional tantrums (like any teenager), and a compulsive masturbator.

ADULTHOOD

Alex is now 33 years old and has a very successful career as a lawyer, and is also the Assistant Commissioner for the City of New

York Commission on Human Opportunity. He lives alone and has a car, which his parents are constantly urging him to get rid of because they think it is too dangerous. Once again, he finds himself leading a double life: his day job is to improve living conditions for the city's most disadvantaged inhabitants, but alongside this he has a chaotic, extreme sex life and treats all the women around him as nothing more than receptors all his anxiety about his job and his family. In spite of his professional success, his parents are still not satisfied, as they want him to settle down with a nice Jewish girl and have Jewish children. The two key episodes of this stage of Alex's life are his relationship with Mary Jane Reed and his trip to Israel.

His relationship with Mary Jane (nicknamed "The Monkey") is characterised by sexual experimentation, as no other woman in New York can match her sexual prowess. However, she also has a number of flaws, many of which stem from her lower-class origins. She climbed out of poverty and became a cosmopolitan woman by letting men treat her as a sexual object, has no desire to grow intellectually or spiritually, and expects

Alex to save her from her own perversions. When he decides that sex alone is not enough and that she is not the woman for him, she threatens to commit suicide, but he pays her no heed and abandons her while they are on holiday together in Europe.

Alex's trip to Israel is a revelation and marks a profound change of direction for him. After finding sexual fulfilment with Mary Jane, he decides to travel to the country to confront his relationship with Judaism, which he thinks has ruined his life, head-on. However, he is taken by surprise by what he finds there: in this majority-Jewish nation, the people are happy, everyone goes to the beach and the women are nothing like the ones he knows back at home. Instead, they are independent and empowered, and know exactly where they are going and what they want. One of these women, Naomi, changes his life when she calls him a coward and forces him to face up to the fact that the "curse" holding him back is merely a figment of his imagination. She sees Judaism as a source of community and freedom, whereas he is nothing more than a pawn in a giant game of chess. Alex retaliates with the only weapon he knows how to use against women: sexual violence. He tries to rape Naomi, but she fights him off and, what is more, he finds that he cannot get an erection. He wonders what this has to do with discovering the truth about life, and the novel closes with him screaming in pain in his psychiatrist's office.

CHARACTER STUDY

ALEXANDER PORTNOY

The novel's protagonist is a 33-year-old lawyer who grew up in the Jewish Weequahic neighbourhood of Newark. All his life, he has tried to live up to his parents' expectations, and was top of his class at school and university. By the time the novel starts, the Mayor of New York has appointed him to a prestigious public office in the city, in spite of his relative youth.

However, his parents still do not seem to be satisfied, as they want him to have children with a Jewish woman in the near future in order to pass on the family's surname and religion. Their pressure forces him to lead a double life: in public, he is a pillar of the community who is trying to change his country for the better by helping disadvantaged groups in his city, but his private life is characterised by sexual excess and compulsive masturbation, which he uses as coping mechanisms to deal with his growing dissatisfaction with life and the anxiety that has brought him to the brink of a nervous breakdown.

SOPHIE GINSKY

Sophie is a stereotypical Jewish mother and seems like a hydra whose tentacles wind their way into every corner of her son's life. On Alex's first day of school, he thought that all his female teachers were his mother in disguise so that she could see how he was behaving and how he acted when she was not around. She lives for her family, especially her children, but this sometimes leads her to meddle in their lives too much.

She is a fantastic cook: she makes jellies with peach slices "just *suspended* there, in defiance of the law of gravity" (p. 11), banana cakes and homemade horseradish (so that she does not have to buy the *pishachs* that come in a bottle), and watches the butcher "like a hawk" (*ibid*.) to make sure he puts her meat through the kosher grinder. She is meticulous and exceptionally demanding when it comes to cleanliness and tidiness: she looks for holes in her children's socks, inspects their bodies and nails for any signs of dirt, and pours cold peroxide into their ears to get to the nooks that cotton buds cannot reach.

There are no lengths that she will not go to in order to eliminate any germs and bodily secretions, and she devotes much of her attention to this task. She also has a particular gift for traumatising her children, as she passes on her own fears that the world is a dangerous place and that death is lurking around every corner, whether in the form of non-Jewish food or meningitis contracted from public swimming pools. However, she is bitter because she feels that nobody, especially not Alex, appreciates all her efforts on their behalf.

JACK PORTNOY

Alex remembers his father being constantly constipated: in the evenings he would take a suppository and read the paper while waiting for what the family referred to as "the miracle" (p. 5). His constipation was so severe that they would even pray in an effort to relieve him from it.

Alex also remembers his father as a hard-working man who has never received the recognition or rewards his efforts deserves. He pours his heart and soul into his work at an insurance company not only to give his family a better future, but also because he truly believes in the insurance policies he is selling. Like Sophie, he sees the world as rife with dangers and potential accidents. For this reason, he even spends his weekends canvassing in impoverished neighbourhoods that are home to "callow Poles, and violent Irishmen, and illiterate Negroes" (p. 7) who are about to lose their insurance policies, jeopardising their families' futures.

Jack symbolises tradition and responsibility, and tells Alex that now that he has turned 30 he has a duty to carry on the family name and preserve the Jewish traditions he has always been so determined to reject.

MARY JANE REED

Mary Jane, also known as "The Monkey", is one of Alex's girlfriends, and his relationship with her is one of his longest. She moved from West Virginia to New York when she was 18. She had no money and no teeth, but was able to afford extensive dental work, as well as trips to Europe and entry into some of the continent's most sophisticated social circles, when she married a

French industrialist. In return, he expected her to fulfil his wildest sexual fantasies, but when these became too extreme she divorced him.

Mary Jane is the only real woman who can live up to Alex's overactive imagination when it comes to sex. His sex life with her is incredible because she is an expert in oral sex, is willing to take part in threesomes and is always ready to have sex, no matter what the circumstances or the location (even the street). However, she is too superficial for Alex's liking and he cannot imagine her as the mother of his children, which is a problem for him even though he insists that he does not want to get married. This all means that he cannot truly fall in love with her. He never tells his parents about her, and not only because she is not Jewish; her ignorance, lack of class and inordinate sensuality, which borders on vulgarity, also play a part in his decision.

HESHIE PORTNOY

Heshie is Alex's cousin, and although he only makes a brief appearance in the novel, he has a major impact on the protagonist's life. He is one of the stars of the school athletics team and a record-breaking javelin thrower. This, and the fact that Heshie is defying his parents' wishes by going out with Alice, the head drum majorette of the school band, who is not Jewish, means that Alex looks up to him. His family think that this relationship brings dishonour on them, so they do everything in their power to keep the young couple apart, even going so far as to claim that Heshie has a terminal illness and lying to Alice so that she will stay away.

Heshie is a significant character because he is the only one who is able to rebel against his father's authority. However, his moment of defiance comes to an end when he lies motionless on the floor and cries for 15 minutes, showing that he has surrendered to his father's will. Alex knows that he only gave up because of his uncle's deceit, and when Heshie died, the only thing his father said was that it was lucky he had not left a non-Jewish wife and children behind. This has a profound impact on Alex, and he never forgets his uncle's words.

NAOMI

Naomi is a young Jewish woman who lives in a commune with other young Israelis near the Syrian border. Alex picks her up when she is hitchhiking to Haifa. She is 21 years old, is nearly six feet tall and originally comes from the US. In terms of personality, she is independent, idealistic and passionate, and has left-wing political leanings. She believes that everybody should be treated equally and have the same opportunities, and is opposed to the way American society works because she thinks that it feeds the darker side of human nature.

Alex's meeting with Naomi is a revelation for him, because for the first time he is able to see a woman as a potential source of salvation rather than merely a sexual object. For him, Naomi is everything that a Jewish woman should be, and, apart from her red hair, she is the polar opposite of Sophie. After she criticises the way he has been living, he is temporarily overcome by madness and proposes to her. She says no because she barely knows him and because she sees him as a coward and a puppet of the system. Alex is furious at her for standing up to him and tries to rape her, but she fights him off thanks to her past training in the military and he finds that he cannot get an erection.

DOCTOR SPIELVOGEL

All we know about Doctor Spielvogel is that he is Alex's psychoanalyst. He does not speak much, his physical appearance is not described and we never find out what he thinks about Alex's behaviour. The only thing we know about him is that his conversations with his patient enable him to diagnose him with a personality disorder which he dubs "Portnoy's Complaint", and about which he writes an article for the *Internationale Zeitschrift für Psychoanalyse*. Similarly, we are never told whether his patient's condition improves over the course of his sessions with him.

ANALYSIS

FORM

The novel is set in Doctor Spielvogel's office, although we are transported to other locations by Alex's memories as he uses his psychoanalysis sessions to try and find an alternative form of catharsis to uninhibited sex and masturbation.

The novel is divided into chapters, but rather than giving it a formal, closed structure, they serve to group the themes of Alex's memories into distinct sections. For example, "Whacking Off" discusses his first adventures in the world of compulsive masturbation, "The Jewish Blues" details his clashes with his parents and his burgeoning opposition to Judaism during his teenage years, and "In Exile" focuses on his impressions of Jewish life in Israel and his discussions and disagreement with Naomi.

These divisions serve more to guide the reader than to structure the narrative. The novel is a monologue stretching over almost 300 pages in which the protagonist complains, tells jokes, throws tantrums and reveals his darkest secrets as he reflects on his dissatisfaction with life, which is the root cause of his unhealthy relationship with sex.

The narrative constantly shifts between the past and the future, and Alex frequently appeals to Spielvogel to save him from his suffering, although we never hear the doctor's response:

> "Doctor, what do you call this sickness I have? Is this the Jewish suffering I used to hear so much about? [...] Doctor, I can't stand any more being frightened like this over nothing! Bless me with manhood! Make me brave! Make me strong! Make me whole!" (p. 37)

STYLE

The fact that the novel takes the form of an extended monologue gives its protagonist the chance to express himself, and he makes full use of this opportunity, right down to the typographical choices. Some passages are written entirely in italics or in capital letters as a way of conveying the intensity of Alex's memories and the extreme anguish they cause him. Alex is fuelled by both rage and lust, and this comes across clearly in the language he uses.

Sex and masturbation are described in explicit terms, but are not always portrayed as sensual experiences; instead, they are often violent and desperate. Alex seems to be consumed by shame and by his burning desire to get as far away from his family and the burden of their expectations as possible.

In a 2014 article for *The New York Times Style Magazine*, Roth discussed the experience of rereading *Portnoy's Complaint* 55 years after it was first published. Of course, looking back on the novel allows the author to adopt a more critical stance towards it, but some things have not changed, and Roth still asserts that the purpose of the repulsive elements in the novel is to demonstrate the fragility of humanity and break free of traditional narrative methods.

Language is a way of discussing the appearance of and revealing the truth behind the more repulsive aspects of life. In the article, Roth explains that "Chekhov [Russian playwright and short story writer, 1860-1904] wisely advised that the writer's task lies not in solving problems but in properly presenting the problem". Psychoanalysis sessions aim to do the same thing: they represent a safe space, almost like a confessional, in which the protagonist is not a sexual deviant, but a person with problems who is seeking help. They provide the perfect setting for Alex's inner world, which has no rules and in which words pour forth unstoppably in a kind of stream of consciousness.

THEMES

Tensions between the Jewish and non-Jewish worlds

Alex is from a Jewish family, which, like any religious environment, has its positive and negative aspects. However, as the novel progresses it becomes clear that there are significant differences between the Jewish world and the *goyische* (non-Jewish) world to which the vast majority of Americans belong. All his life, Alex has been told that not everyone is lucky enough to be born Jewish, and that *goyim* is synonymous with bad, while Jewish is synonymous with good. Indeed, he tells Spielvogel that the first contrast his parents explained to him was not the difference between day and night or hot and cold, but between Jewish and *goyim*.

In a sense, his parents and the Jewish community as a whole have their reasons for thinking this way. Jews were ruthlessly persecuted in Europe during the Second World War (1939-1945), when Alex was just a child, but his family also faced anti-Semitism in the United States. At the start of the novel, the Portnoys become aware that the atmosphere in their New Jersey neighbourhood is starting to change: a swastika appears on the side of one of the buildings, another swastika is carved into the desk of a girl in Alex's sister's class, and Alex's sister is chased by a gang of boys who, we are given to assume, are rabid anti-Semites. Heshie's father has little sympathy for Alex's family: he simply laughs and tells them that this is to be expected if they live in a *goyim* neighbourhood.

Portnoy's Complaint also depicts Jewish pride, as embodied in the expression *goyische naches*, which refers to non-Jewish behaviours or activities, such as military service and sports, that the Jews are proud of not partaking in. They ridicule these types of activities and feel superior because they genuinely do not care whether they win or lose. However, this pride is mingled with a sense of tragedy, which Alex despises and begins to rebel against when he is a teenager. During an argument with his father on Rosh Hashanah (Jewish New Year), Alex says that God does not exist and refuses to dress well for the ceremony, which is seen as shameful for his family and the rest of the Jewish community:

> "'Maybe they don't mean anything because you don't know anything about them, Mr. Big Shot. What do you know about the history of Rosh Hashanah? [...] What do you know about the history of the Jewish people [...] that you can call all that suffering and heartache a lie?'
> [...]
> 'A's in school,' he says, 'but in life he's as ignorant as the day he was born'. Well, it looks as though the time has come at last so I say it. It's something I've known for a little while now. 'You're the ignorant one! You!'" (pp. 61-63)

As we can see, Alex's opposition to his religion is inextricably linked to his disagreements with his parents. We get the impression that he thinks that if he were not Jewish, and if his parents had not given him a Jewish upbringing (he sees their constant fear and guilt at being alive or deserving good things a s inevitable consequences of their religion), his life would be different. For this reason, Alex secretly reveres everything non-Jewish, is overcome with lust when he sees a *shikse* woman, and is stunned when he travels to Israel and encounters Jews who do not share his inhibitions:

> "It is just seven o' clock, yet when I look outside I see the beach already swarming with people. It is a startling sight at such an early hour, particularly as the day is Saturday and I was anticipating a sabbath mood of piety and solemnity to pervade the city. But the crowd of Jews yet again! is gay." (p. 255)

Sexuality and shame

Alex has a tense relationship with his parents, and he believes that this is at least partly due to the fact that they are Jewish. Although Jack and Sophie only want what is best for their son, they impress upon him that the world is full of dangers, tragedies and germs that are lying in wait for unsuspecting victims. They scream "Watch out! Don't do it! Alex no!" (p. 37), and once when he was still a teenager, Sophie demanded to inspect the contents of the toilet to check whether he had been eating chips at school.

They are no less controlling when Alex leaves school to go to university and study law (partly because his parents wanted him to), and later when he is living alone in New York. Among their many complaints and demands, they want him to call and visit them more often, stop driving his car and tell them before he goes on holiday. Although this is typical of many parents, no matter what their nationality or religion, it has a greater effect on Alex than on most people, inspiring contempt and even hatred for his parents because he has spent his entire life trying to make them happy.

To the outside world, Alex appears to be the perfect Jew: he is intelligent and well-educated, and has an excellent job. However, this is still not enough for his parents, because he has not got married or had children yet. Although they do take pride in their son's achievements and enjoy cutting out newspaper clippings, they can always find fault with him, and are pained at his failure to find a wife. This feeling that he will never be good enough has a major impact on Alex's life, and manifests itself above all in his sex life. As Doctor Spielvogel says, "[a]cts of exhibitionism, voyeurism, fetishism, auto-eroticism and oral coitus are plentiful; as a consequence of the patient's 'morality,' however, neither fantasy nor act issues in genuine sexual gratification" (Front Matter). Alex feels as though his penis is the only thing that truly belongs to him, which explains why he masturbates compulsively, starting when he is a teenager and continuing into adulthood.

Alex finds greater pleasure in the fear that somebody will catch him and see how disgusting he really is than in the act itself. For him, sex, especially masturbation, provides catharsis and an escape from the frustrations of the world around him. Ejaculation is far more than a source of sexual pleasure; it makes him feel free and releases him from the burden of his emotional life and his parents.

However, sex and masturbation also make him feel ashamed and guilty: he dreads to think what his parents would say if they knew about his sordid sex life with *shikses*, especially Mary Jane, or how the rest of society would react if they knew about the private life of one of their respected public officials. Although Alex's choice of women is inspired by his desire to defy his father's wishes, he does not want anybody to see him with them, which means that he seeks out women who are exceptionally sexually permissive and who will not expect any kind of commitment from him.

Unlike his public life, which is characterised by perfection but also fear and tragedy, his sex life is all about experimentation and degradation as he tries to become a real man and escape from the "Jewish joke" (p. 36) that is his life. He is constantly ashamed and feels that he is never good enough, but ultimately his sexual escapades do nothing to assuage these emotions.

The role of women

In the same way that the world is divided into a Jewish part and a *goyische* part, for Alex women also fall into one of two categories: they either play the role of the mother (Jewish women) or serve as mere objects for the fulfilment of men's deepest sexual desires (non-Jewish women).

These roles seem to be interchangeable to an extent: although Alex's relationship with his mother is fraught and she is omnipresent, given to blackmail, fatalistic and overly protective, in a way she is the first woman he is intimate with. When he was a child, and even as an adult, she would put her stockings on in front of him, and on one occasion she asked him to watch her in front of his father, who was excluded from this "mother and son" ritual. Sophie was also the person who taught him to use the toilet, and in doing so would stroke his penis, which she referred to as his "little thing" (p. 50). Understandably, these episodes had a lasting impact on Alex.

He always conflates other Jewish women with his mother, which serves to explain his fixation on *shikse* women: because they are not part of the Jewish world, they can never be like Sophie. Instead, they are sexual objects for his enjoyment. Alex sees the world as filled with possibilities, and, unlike his mother, non-Jewish women see him as a man and a sexual being. This can be seen in his relationship with Mary Jane, who is the only woman who is able to fulfil his sexual desires but who proves unsatisfying in other areas.

Perhaps surprisingly, deep down Alex wants to find a woman who will live up to his parents' expectations, meaning a woman who shares his religion, is intelligent, attractive and modest, and is nothing like his mother. In spite of his apparent contempt for the Jewish world, he actually yearns to fit in there. Towards the end of the novel, he confesses that he dreams of coming home from a softball match on a Sunday to a wife who is preparing a meal for them and his parents. In short, he longs for a simple, peaceful family life with a loving wife and children.

His trip to Israel is a revelation for him. In this country, the majority of the population are Jews and he is introduced to a different side to his religion, which is perhaps less orthodox and fatalistic than Judaism as it is practised in Newark. His brief meeting with Naomi changes his life. This red-haired, freckled, innocent, idealistic Jewish woman shares many of the passionate convictions about justice that he held in his younger days and believes in the idea of a fair society and a common struggle. However, she mistrusts him, as, unlike women such as Mary Jane, she is not looking for sex or for somebody to rescue her from her own perversions. When he unexpectedly proposes to her, she turns him down because she knows that he is broken inside, is consumed by self-loathing and needs help. She is brutally frank, and tells him that his tragedies are "[n]ot Jewish humor!", but rather "[g]hetto humor", which is shared by the Jewish diaspora (p. 265). This leads to an argument, in the course of which Alex becomes enraged and tries to rape her, as this is the only way he can assert his dominance. However, Naomi has previously undertaken military training and is able to fight him off; meanwhile, Alex cannot get an erection. This problem continues for the rest of his stay in Israel, which is what motivates him to go see a psychiatrist.

FURTHER REFLECTION

SOME QUESTIONS TO THINK ABOUT...

- Why do you think *Portnoy's Complaint* was so controversial when it was first published? Explain at least three elements that could have scandalised readers.
- What is Doctor Spielvogel's role in the novel?
- What role does masturbation play in Alex's life?
- How can remembering the past help Alex to change his future?
- Do you think Alex's life would have been different if he was not from a Jewish family? Justify your answer.
- What is the role of the public and the private in the novel?
- What does Alex discover during his trip to Israel?
- Why is Alex's brief meeting with Naomi so important to him?
- What does Alex mean when he says that his life is a "Jewish joke" (p. 36)?

- Can you think of any other examples of the stereotype of the Jewish mother in books, films or television?
- Why is Alex unable to get an erection in Israel?

We want to hear from you!
Leave a comment on your online library
and share your favourite books on social media!

FURTHER READING

REFERENCE EDITION

- Roth, P. (1994) *Portnoy's Complaint*. New York: Vintage.

REFERENCE STUDIES

- Gross, B. (1981) Seduction of the Innocent: *Portnoy's Complaint* and Popular Culture. *MELUS*. 5(8). [Online]. [Accessed 5 April 2018]. Available from: <http://www.jstor.org/stable/467391?seq=1#page_scan_tab_contents>

- Roth, P. (2014) Old Books, New Thoughts. *The New York Times Style Magazine*. [Online]. [Accessed 5 April 2018]. Available from: <https://www.nytimes.com/2014/11/06/t-magazine/pen-auction-philip-roth.html>

RECOMMENDED READING

- Posnok, R. (2008) *Philip Roth's Rude Truth: The Art of Immaturity*. Princeton: Princeton University Press.

- Statlander, J. (2011) *Philip Roth's Postmodern American Romance: Critical Essays on Selected Works*. New York: Peter Lang.

ADAPTATION

- *Portnoy's Complaint*. (1972) [Film]. Ernst Lehman. Dir. USA: Warner Brothers.

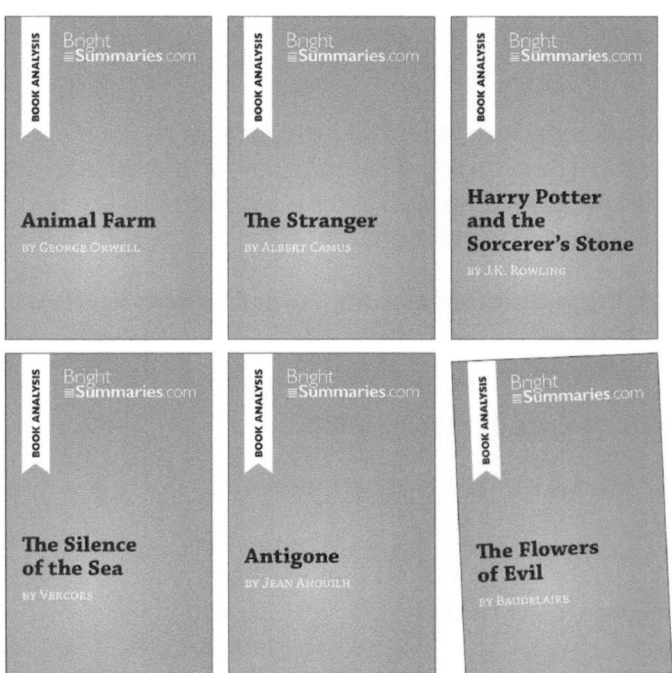

www.brightsummaries.com

Ebook EAN: 9782808001908

Paperback EAN: 9782808009195

Legal Deposit: D/2018/12603/218

Cover: © Primento

Digital conception by Primento, the digital partner of publishers.